W9-AJU-997

THE TOHONO O'ODHAM

JACQUELINE D. GREENE

THE TOHONO O'ODHAM

Franklin Watts   A Division of Grolier Publishing
New York   London   Hong Kong   Sydney   Danbury, Connecticut
A First Book

Acknowledgements

The author wishes to thank Diane and Randy Graham of the Papago Trading Post for their willing assistance with information and photo opportunities, and for extending the hand of friendship. Special thanks also to teacher Margie Butler and Sister Carol of the San Xavier Reservation Mission School for their welcome assistance.

Title page photo: A dancer in face paint and feathered regalia waits to dance at the annual Tohono O'odham Powwow at San Xavier Reservation.

Map by Joe LeMonnier
Photographs ©: Arizona Historical Society: 11, 30, 32, 33, 46 (Tucson); Arizona State Museum: 19, 29, 38, 55, 57, 35 (E.W. Haury), 27 (Helga Teiwes); Art Resource: 24 (National Museum of American Art, Washington D.C.); First Image West: 25 (Ken Akers); Jacqueline Dembar Greene: cover, 8, 9, 13, 14, 16, 20, 22, 37, 39, 42, 43, 44, 48, 53; Photo Researchers: 18 (Francois Gohier); Visuals Unlimited: 6 (Doug Sokell).

Visit Franklin Watts on the Internet at:
http://publishing.grolier.com

Library of Congress Cataloging-in-Publication Data
Greene, Jacqueline Dembar.
The Tohono O'odham / Jacqueline D. Greene.
p.   cm.—(A first book)
Includes bibliographical references and index.
Summary: Examines the history, culture, daily life, and current situation of the Tohono O'odham, whose name means "the Desert People."
ISBN 0-531-20326-3 (lib. bdg.)   0-531-15912-4 (pbk.)
1. Tohono O'odham Indians—History—Juvenile literature. 2. Tohono O'odham Indians—Social life and customs—Juvenile literature. [1. Tohono O'odham Indians. 2. Indians of North America.] I. Title. II. Series.
E99.P25G74   1998
970'.0049745—dc21   97-11688
                                                                            CIP
                                                                            AC

© 1998 Jacqueline Dembar Greene
All rights reserved. Published simultaneously in Canada
Printed in the United States of America
1 2 3 4 5 6 7 8 9 10 R 07 06 05 04 03 02 01 00 99 98

CONTENTS

SUNRISE HIGHLIGHTS GIANT SAGUARO, PRICKLY CHOLLA,
AND OTHER DESERT CACTI.

LIFE IN THE DESERT

The chill night air covers the desert in the hours before the sun rises and heats the sand and everything that walks upon it. A father's soft voice awakens his children. His daughter blinks her eyes in the darkness, and her brother sits up on his sleeping mat.

"The day is coming and there is much to do. Today you must run fast, like Brother Coyote. You, young daughter, must fetch water and grind corn to make the family strong. My son, you must learn to accept the heat and your thirst without complaint. You must do this for the Desert People."

For hundreds of years, this is how the people of the arid Sonoran Desert awoke. The northern Pima tribe called them *Pavi O'odham,* meaning the Bean People, because they grew crops of beans. Spanish explorers arrived in the 1600s and mispronounced the name as Papago. In 1983, the tribe reaffirmed its traditional name and officially became *Tohono O'odham* (TOH-na OH-tahm), the Desert People, or simply *O'odham,* the People.

YELLOW CHOLLA BLOSSOMS LATER GROW INTO FRUIT.
TOHONO WOMEN CAREFULLY PICK THEM WITH WOOD TONGS.

When the Spanish first made contact with them, these desert dwellers occupied land that stretched for thousands of miles across what is now southern Arizona and northwestern Mexico. The Spanish called this area the *Papaguería*, land of the Papago.

The O'odham learned to tolerate the extreme temperature changes of the Sonoran Desert. During winter, sunny days can bring mild temperatures, but at night the air can grow as cold as 15° F (-9° C), and snow is common in the nearby mountains. In summer, temperatures rise as high as 120° F (49° C) but fall to 50° F (10° C) at night. Only 5 to 15 inches (13 to 38 cm) of rain will fall each year, but heavy downpours can flood fields, and at other times severe droughts can threaten the survival of crops. The plants and animals that survive in this climate need little rain.

Finding water and keeping a daily supply was a difficult task, and not a drop could be wasted. A few Tohono O'odham lived near desert oases and didn't have to travel far to fill their water jugs. But young girls often traveled many miles into the mountains to collect the day's water. The men found low spots in the desert that naturally collected rainwater and dug them deeper with wooden sticks. These *charcos* can still be seen on tribal lands. Like their ancestors, the men dug vast irrigation ditches. They also made brush dams at the mouths of sandy stream beds called *arroyos*. When rains came, water collected behind the dams and could be redirected onto fields as it was needed.

AFTER THE RAIN, WATER RUSHES DOWN THE MOUNTAINS
AND FILLS DRY BEDS SUCH AS THIS ARROYO.

RANCHES AND RAMADAS

The Tohono O'odham lived on isolated ranches. The largest villages of about 250 people might have as many as forty ranch houses spread across several miles and connected by desert trails.

Villages ➤ The most important relationship in each person's life was with the family. Next came close attachments to the village, where most residents were related. Work and food were always shared, for if one person was hungry or weak, everyone suffered. Whenever there was a threat to the tribe, villages banded together for protection.

People loved to visit and would walk long distances between ranches. It was common for women to show up at a cousin's house carrying a cotton blanket to sit on and some work to be completed. Talking softly together, they plaited sleeping mats, wove a basket, or ground corn into meal. Whenever visitors arrived, the host welcomed them with a drink of water and presented them with a small gift of food before they left.

PEOPLE IN TOHONO VILLAGES RELY ON EACH OTHER FOR SURVIVAL. THESE MEN WORK TOGETHER TO BUILD A TRADITIONAL HOUSE

Men worked in groups to farm or to build houses. Occasionally they hunted together, but whenever one killed a large animal, he shared the meat with everyone.

The eldest village members had the most authority. Usually one man was elected to lead council meetings. Men met in a round Council House and talked about a problem until everyone agreed on the solution.

People moved to different locations depending on the season and the food available. In June, they traveled to *cactus camps*, temporary sites set up among the giant saguaro, where they spent a few weeks gathering and cooking the sweet fruit that grew at the tops of the 50-foot-high (15-m) plants. They lived in their village houses in the late spring and winter and remained there until crops were planted and growing well. During the hot summer, the O'odham traveled to cooler mountain valleys. They often made trips higher up the mountains to collect acorns, pine nuts, and edible grasses.

Houses ➤ When a family was ready to build a home, members cleared an area of land, often with help from others in the village. They planted *mesquite trees* and *creosote bushes* to give shade in summer, and the mesquite beans could be ground into flour. Sometimes the yard was fenced with thin ribs from dead cacti to keep out wild animals.

Most houses were low, round domes with one main room. The walls were made of thin *ocotillo* cactus, which often took root and sprouted leaves and bright red blossoms. Sometimes grasses were woven through the open walls for extra protection from weather, small animals, and insects. The roof was thatched with grass or brush. Men dug a pit in the center of the house for

PRICKLY FENCES MADE OF OCOTILLO CACTUS SOMETIMES TAKE ROOT AND SPROUT RED BLOSSOMS.

a fire, which provided light and heat on cold winter nights. O'odham homes didn't have a smoke hole in the roof because smoke could easily escape through the open doorway and spaces in the walls. At night, each member of the family slept on a woven grass mat that was pushed against the wall to help keep out bugs. They didn't use blankets, so if the night was cold, they kept a fire burning.

Every house had an open, covered area attached to it called a *ramada*. Mesquite wood posts held up a flat thatched roof, and the ground underneath was swept clean every day. In summer, the family slept under the

LATER TOHONO HOMES HAD MUD WALLS IN THE MEXICAN STYLE, BUT ALL HAD AN ATTACHED, SHADED RAMADA.

ramada to catch the cool breezes. During the day, women cooked and worked under its shade. The family's pots, baskets, and gourds were neatly stacked. A large *olla,* a special clay jug that kept water cool, was filled each morning. It was kept under the ramada for cooking or offering a precious drink to visitors.

The roofs of the houses were not strong enough to keep out heavy summer rains. As time went on, the O'odham tried wood, tar paper, and tin. By the 1900s, many began building Mexican-style homes with walls made of mud plaster. Some built homes of *adobe,* but this was expensive, as someone from outside the village had to be hired to bring in the bricks.

CEREMONIES AND BATTLES

The Tohono O'odham believe they were created by *I'itoi,* Elder Brother, who brought them from the earth through a sacred cave nestled in the foothills of the Baboquivari Mountains. After I'itoi created the people, he gave them all the edible plants of the desert and taught them how to prepare each one. He sang songs to protect the tribe from its enemies and showed them the power of singing.

Songs and Stories ➤ Men and women had dreams or visions in which they would hear a song, and men who learned ceremonial songs were greatly respected. Each song was like a poem with repeated verses describing dreams and wishes. Mothers sang to help their children grow strong. Men sang to find and kill animals or gain power over their enemies. They sang to bring summer rains and insure a good harvest.

Medicine men were members of the tribe who were given a special message from the animal world. They could cure illnesses and communicate with

THE SACRED MOUNTAIN OF BABOQUIVARI PEAK RISES
FROM THE DESERT NEAR TOPAWA. LEGEND TELLS THAT
THE GOD I'ITOI BROUGHT THE TOHONO O'ODHAM
PEOPLE FROM A CAVE UNDER THIS PEAK.

spirits of the dead, who might appear in the form of an owl. Some could predict the future.

The number four had special significance, perhaps because of the four directions of the earth. Every winter, a storyteller recited the creation story over four days and nights. All the men gathered in the Council House and sat in a ceremonial cross-legged position with their arms folded across their chests and heads bent down. Storytellers spent years learning the long, complicated legend, as not a single word could be changed. Because the O'odham didn't have written language, legends had to be passed down orally.

Every four years there was a fall harvest celebration called *Viikita*, held with the Pima tribe. For months, villages prepared songs and designed masks and elaborate costumes. Groups made floats and presented dramas. The event lasted four days and four nights.

Rain Ceremony ➡ The most important ritual of the year was the cactus wine ceremony, which was believed to have the power to bring rain. Late spring marked the beginning of the O'odham year, when everyone moved to their cactus camps and prepared for the Rain Magic of this ceremony.

In late May or early June, the white blossoms at the tops of the saguaro turned to red pear-shaped fruit. The women alerted the village that it was time to "make rain." In a spirit of celebration, everyone gathered cooking pots, sleeping mats, and dried corn and headed off to the saguaro stands.

Each family set up a campsite in the shade of rocky ledges or under a quickly built ramada. Women used long wood poles to knock the fruit to the ground. Often it would split open when it fell. Children scooped out the juicy red pulp. They left the empty shells on the ground facing the sky because their grandmothers told them this would help bring rain.

The fruit was boiled in large pots of water and then strained through a fine grass mat. The cooled

WOMEN USE LONG POLES TO KNOCK FRUIT OFF HIGH SAGUARO BRANCHES.

syrup was poured into clay jugs and closed with a stopper made of wadded grass. Many elders say that when they went to sleep under the stars, they felt the first drops of rain.

When all the fruit had been cooked, people carried the jugs of syrup home in nets on their backs. Every family contributed a few jars for the rain ceremony. These were collected in the Council House, which was then called the Rain House, and poured into four large jugs. The Medicine Men watched over the syrup until it fermented. Then one person walked through the village, singing, "Come together. The fire is glowing, the sun is setting, and it is time to call down the rain."

The entire village danced, and speeches were recited in the same words used by the O'odhams' ancestors. Then four young men passed among the male members of the group, holding tightly woven baskets filled with the special wine. Each man sang a traditional song and drank from the basket. Most of them became mildly intoxicated. This, however, was considered a holy state, in which each man was purified and dreamed songs he later shared. It was the only time during the year that anyone drank wine.

SAGUARO FRUIT IS COOKED INTO SYRUP AND THEN STRAINED. LEFTOVER SEEDS ARE GROUND INTO FLOUR.

THREE YOUNG WOMEN DANCE IN THE OPENING
PROCESSION AT THE ANNUAL TOHONO O'ODHAM POWWOW.

At the end of the fourth night of the wine ceremony, as people returned to their ranches, elders say
there would be a rainstorm. The Desert People were
filled with happiness, knowing their crops would
grow. When the rain came, it filled the charcos and
washed down the arroyos, soaking the fields. This was
the Rain Magic of the Tohono O'odham.

Puberty ➡ Boys had no formal puberty rites, but when a girl was about thirteen years old, there was a village celebration. The girl and her friends danced ritual dances late into the night, and she gave gifts of beads and baskets. At the end of the month, she was given a ritual purification bath and went to the Medicine Man. She drank a ceremonial white clay potion, and if the Medicine Man had dreamed it, he gave her a new name.

After the ceremonies, the mother cut her daughter's hair to shoulder length. Playthings were put away and the young woman modeled her behavior after the adult women in the household.

Death ➡ When someone died, there was sadness mixed with the belief that the person would live a happy life in the spirit world. The body was wrapped in cotton cloth and buried in a cave or in the ground, covered with rocks and branches. The person's favorite possessions were buried with him or her. The family also left food to nourish the person on the journey to the spirit world. After people died, it was considered dangerous to speak their names. Instead, they might be called "brother-gone" or "grandmother-gone," according to their relationship to the speaker.

War ➡ The Tohono O'odham hated war and saw it as a terrible thing. They never fought against white

THIS BASKET SHOWS THE MAZE OF THE GOD I'ITOI.
ACCORDING TO LEGEND, I'ITOI ENTERS THE PATH OF LIFE
WITH ITS MANY FALSE PASSAGES. WHEN HIS JOURNEY IS
COMPLETE, HE RESTS BEFORE MEETING HIS DEATH.

settlers. Their only declared enemies were the Apache, who constantly attacked their fields and villages, killing the men, stealing horses and crops, and taking women and children captive. Children were taught to be fast runners, in case they had to make a sudden escape. Men kept bows and arrows with them at all times, even while working in the fields.

Battle Plans → When the people in a village felt threatened by a nearby Apache encampment or needed to retaliate for an earlier attack, men met in the Council House. A respected elder, called the Keeper of the Smoke, prepared a fire and led the discussion. If everyone agreed on a raid, the Keeper of the Smoke would ask who wished to participate. Men didn't become warriors to seek glory or prove their bravery. They believed it was their duty to endure the risk of battle to protect their family and village. Each young man volunteered willingly.

Swift runners went to nearby villages asking for help. A notched stick showed how many days would pass until the war party left. On the appointed day, men from different villages arrived and prepared to fight.

Although they tried to avoid war, O'odham men constantly prepared for the possibility. They made arrows and sharpened quartz stones that were believed to hold powerful magic. Warriors carried as many as one hundred arrows on a raid, a strong bow, a heavy war club, and a buckskin shield.

The night before the war party left, the Medicine Man asked the owls for the spirits' help in the coming battle. One man was chosen leader. He told stories of successful raids as a charm to bring victory. There was no dancing or yelling among the men. Warriors who had been on past raids sang songs they believed would take away their enemy's power.

BLACK KNIFE, AN 1846 PAINTING OF AN APACHE WARRIOR,
BY JOHN MIX STANLEY.

When the morning star rose in the dark sky, the party began their journey to the enemy camp. The men coated their skin with grease as protection against the cold nights and wore straw sandals during the long march. They painted their faces with red and black lines, and most tied their long hair into a knot.

The men carried other items attached to their belts. Each had a pouch filled with black paint, a small olla filled with drinking water, a sack of parched corn, and a dried gourd. They didn't cook while on the trail so their enemies wouldn't see any smoke. They ate *pinole*, a mixture of dried corn and water.

The war party traveled at night and attacked just as dawn broke, to surprise the Apache. The Tohono O'odham did not steal anything or take prisoners. They believed the Apache and all their possessions contained powerful forces of evil.

Enemy Slayers ➤ As soon as a Tohono O'odham warrior killed an enemy, he became an Enemy Slayer.

AFTER SUNSET, THE WAR PARTY COULD TRAVEL UNDETECTED ACROSS THE OPEN LAND OF THE SONORAN DESERT.

He cut a lock of hair from his victim, took one of his moccasins, and left the battlefield. He blackened his face with paint from his waist pouch. It was the first step in an important purification process to protect the warrior from the dangerous power he was believed to have released from his victim. The entire ceremony lasted sixteen days, a multiple of the sacred number four.

The wife of an Enemy Slayer retreated to a small brush hut. A friend took care of her children and brought her food. Children had to be very quiet during the time their father was being purified and stay away from him to prevent the enemy's released power from making them sick.

For sixteen days, the people danced and sang and listened to tales of the battle. But each Enemy Slayer sat alone under a tree, waiting for a vision to give him a new song filled with power. It was his behavior during this difficult time that showed his true strength and bravery. Every four days, an Enemy Slayer, his wife, and his children were given purifying baths in the cold hours of the early morning. With each bath, more of the dangerous enemy power was washed away.

On the last night of the ceremony, other villages joined the events. Young men danced a warrior's dance, filled with high steps and energetic movements, to honor members of the war party. The

MUSIC WAS AN IMPORTANT PART OF MANY
CEREMONIES AND EVENTS.

Enemy Slayers' families gave the dancers food and gifts. Baskets, beads, deerskins, and pottery were common presents, as were horses and cattle. Finally, just before dawn, each Enemy Slayer and his family received one last ritual bath; the enemy's power had been tamed.

An elder fashioned the hair lock a warrior had taken into a small human figure. It was dressed in a fringed buckskin shirt and Apache-style moccasins. It was wrapped in a basket and tucked into the thatch of the roof. Now the family could use the enemy's power to endure thirst, hunger, or cold.

FAMILY LIFE

A Tohono O'odham family often consisted of three generations living together. A son who married brought his wife to live in his parents' household. Families were always willing to take in other relatives, as long as the new members helped with the work. Orphaned cousins, children of divorced parents, and relatives from other villages were welcomed.

Although most family decisions were made after lengthy discussions in which everyone expressed an opinion, a grandfather was head of the household. If he died, the grandmother became the family's leader. If there were no grandparents in the family, it was headed by the son who was considered the wisest.

Marriage ➤ Marriages were arranged by a girl's parents, usually with a young man from a different village. Neither one was consulted beforehand. A father woke his daughter and quietly told her whom she was to marry. He advised her to obey her husband and to work hard.

FAMILIES TYPICALLY SPAN THREE GENERATIONS. GRANDPARENTS PASSED DOWN SKILLS AND WISDOM.

After a couple married, the groom spent four days with his bride at her family's house. Then they went to live with his parents. If a wife's family had no sons and the husband's had many, the couple might remain with the woman's household in order to be the most help.

Children → With the birth of her first child, a woman was considered a full member of her husband's family. When a baby was four weeks old, the parents brought him or her to the Medicine Man. At dawn, the Medicine Man drew a large circle on the ground. The mother and baby, and sometimes the father, sat in the center facing east.

As the sun rose, the Medicine Man waved a sacred bundle of eagle feathers over them. Then he gave the parents a ceremonial drink made with white clay. Finally, he gave the baby a name he had dreamed. This name was thought to have magical power. It was known only by the child and its parents and was almost never used.

Infants were simply called "baby." As they grew older, they were given nicknames that had something to do with their interests or personality, or an unusual experience. Children were mostly called by their family relationship, such as "daughter," "cousin," or "brother."

INFANTS HAD SPECIAL HAMMOCKS UNDER THE SHADE OF THE RAMADA, CLOSE TO THEIR MOTHERS.

Adults were affectionate toward children and held them often. While a mother worked, she rocked her baby in a low hammock. Whenever she traveled, she carried the baby in her arms. At night, very young children slept nestled between their parents.

Children did not have any formal schooling. Grandparents told humorous tales of the legendary wily coyote that showed children the correct way to behave. Kindness, patience, and respect for elders were praised. A parent never hit a child, and a scolding was serious punishment.

By age five, children began to share in household chores. They were encouraged to do whatever they could, even if it was only carrying a stick or a basket.

A girl's most important task was fetching the day's supply of water. Traveling with a group, she set off in the predawn darkness with two empty water jugs in a backpack made of sticks and string netting. Each olla held several gallons of water, and girls traveled swiftly to the closest charco to fill them, then ran back to the house. When water was scarce, they ran for many hours into the mountains. They were always careful not to spill one drop and to return by dawn so the men could eat breakfast before going to the fields. Girls brought wood from the woodpile, kept the floor swept clean, rolled up sleeping mats in the morning, cleaned dishes, and learned to grind flour and to cook.

BOYS TOOK GREAT PRIDE IN THEIR SKILLS AS RIDERS AND
ENJOYED VISITING NEIGHBORING VILLAGES ON HORSEBACK.

Boys chopped wood, fed the animals, and
worked in the fields. They learned to ride horses and
rope calves and would often practice roping a fence
post or an unsuspecting chicken. When they were
quite small, boys would lead a family horse around
the yard, pet it, and groom it. Once they became
skillful riders, they looked forward to the day the men
invited them to help round up cattle.

By the time a boy was about eleven years old, his
father and grandfather had taught him about crops and
animals by telling stories, singing traditional songs, and
showing him how they did things. A son became quite

close to his father. Older boys made friends in other villages and rode off on their horses to visit, small ollas of water hanging at the backs of their saddles.

Daily Life ➔ Breakfast each morning was ground seeds mixed with water, or boiled squash rind. The bowls weren't washed because water could not be spared. Instead, family members scraped the last bit of food from their bowls with their fingers and scrubbed the bowls with sand. Then they washed themselves over a clay bowl filled with a small amount of water.

Before the sun was up, men and boys went to the fields. Women, girls, and small children stayed close to home. Women cut and dried corn, beans,

MUCH OF DAILY LIFE FOR WOMEN AND GIRLS TOOK PLACE CLOSE TO HOME. WOMEN ALSO SPENT HOURS MAKING BEAUTIFUL BASKETS.

and squash and stored them in clay pots buried under the sand for winter use. In the evenings, everyone sat under the ramada until it grew dark. Women usually worked on weaving a basket, a project that could last weeks or even months. Men made bows, arrows, and quartz points. They also braided ropes from agave fibers and made leather pouches and harnesses.

Clothes ➤ In the earliest times, young children wore no clothes. The weather was hot, cloth was scarce, and clothes had to be washed in precious water. As boys and girls grew older, they wore strips of cotton tied around their waists with string. Girls painted the upper part of their bodies red, which was considered beautiful. Almost everyone went barefoot except when traveling long distances, when they wore woven straw sandals.

By the late 1700s, as the Desert People made more contact with the Spanish, they began to wear cotton clothes. Women and girls wore Mexican-style skirts and blouses; men and boys wore trousers and shirts.

Manners ➤ A visitor will always hear laughter when villagers and family members are together. The O'odham have a good sense of humor, and teasing and joking are a part of daily life. Although families lived in close quarters, each person tried to respect others' privacy. It was considered rude to ask direct, personal questions. Children did not interrupt their

PEOPLE WORKED HARD TO SURVIVE IN THE DESERT, BUT ALWAYS WILLINGLY. THESE YOUNG WOMEN HELP HARVEST SAGUARO FRUIT.

elders or ask for help. If adults or older children saw there was a problem, they would simply work alongside a youngster until a task was accomplished.

Although the O'odham language does not have a formal word for "thank you," people gave gifts to each other to express gratitude or simply for the pleasure of making another person happy. The recipient did not thank the giver directly, but instead eventually did a favor in return.

DESERT FOODS

Crops ➤ After the rain ceremony, when the earth was soft and wet, men walked through the fields singing corn songs. They made holes with sharp sticks and dropped four seeds in each. Women covered the holes by pushing the dirt over them with their feet. O'odham also planted tepary beans, which grow well in the dry climate, striped cushaw squash (today called "Indian squash"), and *devil's claw*. The Spanish introduced melons, which added moisture to the diet.

Men and boys watered the plants, kept rodents away, and pulled weeds. When summer came and the crops were growing well, families moved into the cool mountains. They stayed there until harvest time in September and October.

In winter, gentle rains meant the O'odham could plant a second small crop. In the late 1600s, a Spanish missionary, Father Kino, introduced new varieties of winter wheat, peas, lentils, and garbanzo beans, which supplemented the yearly harvest.

A FARMER SELLS PUMPKINS, MELONS, AND CUSHAW
SQUASH IN THE TRIBAL CAPITAL OF SELLS, ARIZONA.

Hunting ➤ Small animals added variety to the diet.
Rabbits were plentiful, as were gophers, birds, and
rattlesnakes. In the mountains, hunters tracked deer,
antelope, bighorn sheep, and occasionally a bear,
wolf, or wildcat.

Some men specialized in hunting deer and were
thought to have spiritual power. A boy who wanted
to be a deer hunter spent several years learning to
make strong arrows and chip stone points. He did
not hunt at first, but he accompanied the men, called
head-bearers because of the deer heads they wore as a
disguise. Covered by deer skins, they would creep

BECAUSE OF THE WARM CLIMATE, THE TOHONO COULD
HARVEST TWO WHEAT CROPS EACH YEAR.

toward their prey on all fours. When a young man killed his first deer, he presented it to his teacher as a gift. He did not eat any of the meat. The head and hide were made into a headdress for him to wear on future hunts. When a deer was killed, it was shared with all the village, but the hunter kept the tail, which held magical powers.

The O'odham were skillful at gathering wild food from the desert, such as chili peppers, wolfberries, wild onions, mesquite beans, and gourds. In late spring, they collected the green buds that grew on cholla cactus. They picked the prickly fruit with cactus rib tongs and rolled them in the sand until the thorns rubbed off. Buds were roasted overnight in a deep pit,

THE FRUIT OF THE PRICKLY PEAR CACTUS HAD TO BE PICKED WITH CARE. THE THORNS WERE REMOVED AND THE BUDS ROASTED BEFORE BEING EATEN.

then dried and stored. Women also traveled into the mountains to gather acorns, roots, and pine nuts.

Salt ➤ To collect salt, which was used as flavoring in cooking and traded with other tribes, O'odham men made a difficult ceremonial four-day journey to the Gulf of California. Their first sight of the ocean was an awe-inspiring experience. Salt was collected along the shore in bags, and then each man conquered his fears and waded into the surf, scattering grains of corn on the water.

Trade ➤ Because the O'odham traveled long distances to hunt and collect salt and wild foods, they became important traders. The Pima spent all of their time tending their fields and welcomed items the O'odham could provide. The most desirable food was the sweet cactus syrup, which the Desert People poured into ollas the Pima could use later for storing water. In return, the Pima gave their southern neighbors squash, corn, beans, and wheat, which the O'odham depended on during times of drought or between harvests.

Tohono O'odham also traded with the Hopi and Pueblo people and with southern tribes in Mexico and Central America. Tribes near the ocean offered shells, skins from jungle animals, and bright-feathered macaws that were kept as pets.

CRAFTS AND GAMES

Of their few possessions, baskets were the O'odhams' most useful and beautiful items. Made using ancient techniques, the baskets were known for their sturdy and artistic designs. They were light enough to carry easily and strong enough to last many years. Today, Tohono O'odham baskets are mainly decorative, but skilled weavers produce more baskets than all other American Indian tribes combined, and the oldest baskets are priceless works of art.

Basket Making ➜ Women gathered yucca leaves, wheat straw, or beargrass, dried them in the sun, and wove them into baskets along with strips of mesquite bark. Some weavers used thin willow branches or sturdy devil's claw, which made a basket so tightly woven it could hold water. Baskets were also sturdy enough to use for cooking with coals.

Girls learned basket making by watching others and then were given materials of their own. A young girl always gave her first basket to the woman who helped her learn.

THE LONG, THIN LEAVES OF THE YUCCA PLANT ARE
DRIED FOR USE IN MAKING STRONG BASKETS.

Elizabeth Rios, a basket maker who lives near Tucson, Arizona, said she learned by watching her aunt. She made her first basket when she was just five years old. Annette Eleando, another O'odham basket maker, learned from her grandmother. She still goes into the desert to pick special grasses, wearing gloves to protect her hands from the sharp tips and edges. She grows her own devil's claw for designs.

O'odham baskets have become collectors' items. In 1971, Rufina Morris, from the San Xavier reservation, made a basket that was presented to Pope Paul VI. Annie Antone, a basket maker from Gila Bend reserva-

BASKET WEAVER ANNETTE ELEANDO (LEFT) HOLDS A COVERED BASKET
MADE WITH THE WHEAT STITCH PATTERN. BEHIND HER IS A BUNDLE OF
BEAR GRASS. ANNETTE MADE HER FIRST BASKET WHEN SHE WAS EIGHT
YEARS OLD. THE TANGLED ROOTS OF THE RARE DEVIL'S CLAW (RIGHT)
ARE USED FOR THE BLACK PATTERNS IN BASKET DESIGNS.

tion, went to the Smithsonian Institution in Washington, D.C., in 1992 to demonstrate her techniques, and she presented one of her baskets for display.

Pottery ➡ O'odham potters were best known for their ollas, which could be as small as a dipper or large enough to hold 10 gallons (38 l) of water. Women sometimes made a tiny olla for a child in the shape of an animal or bird.

Men dug clay early in spring and sifted out small rocks and debris. Women mixed the clay with water until it was soft enough to shape. After they formed a

TOHONO O'ODHAM MOTHERS OFTEN MADE SMALL OLLAS FEATURING BIRD OR ANIMAL HEADS FOR THEIR CHILDREN.

pot, they smoothed it with a wooden paddle. The wet pot dried in the shade and then was fired—baked in a pit with burning wood. Next, women used feathers or leaves to paint designs with black paint mixed from bark and pitch. The pot was fired again, which made the paint burn to a hard, shiny glaze.

Games ➤ O'odham people enjoyed games and always made time for them. Running was probably the most important sport. Girls could already run long distances to collect water, and everyone had to be able to run fast to escape from enemies. Men cleared a track and kept it free of thorns so that children could run barefoot. Villages challenged each other to races. Men raced against men, and women against women. Spectators placed bets on who would win each race. In one popular event, two teams of racers kicked a hard mesquite wood ball over a 10- to 15-mile (16-24 km) race course. Day-long relay races were also big events.

Women played an exciting game called *toka*, similar to field hockey. Players hit a rawhide or wooden ball with long, hooked mesquite sticks toward goals at either end of a field. The game is still played and is a popular school sport.

Gambling was a favorite pastime. The most common game for men was played with wooden throw-

THIS PHOTOGRAPH FROM 1941 SHOWS WOMEN
PLAYING THE TRADITIONAL GAME CALLED TOKA.

ing sticks similar to dice. Markings on the sticks indicated how many steps the player could make around a circle drawn on the ground. Women played a game in which they tossed four painted sticks to win points. People bet mats, blankets, shells, and beads.

Children played with dolls made from mesquite leaves and string. Boys made male dolls and pretended they were on a hunt. Girls made female dolls, set them in front of a small *metate,* or grinding stone, and pretended they were grinding corn.

MISSIONARIES, APACHES, AND AMERICANS

Beginning in 1698, contact with outsiders began to change the Desert People's way of life. Father Kino wrote in his journals that the "Papago" were friendly and willing to learn about the Catholic religion. He tried to improve their lives by giving them seeds, cattle, and horses. Missionaries on the Papaguería taught them to ride and to care for their animals.

The Spanish gave them some metal tools, and O'odham carved wooden copies of the plows and shovels. They took great pleasure in owning horses, which allowed them to visit distant villages, work, and trade. For the first time, they began to think in terms of ownership.

The habit of trading work for food also changed. At first, when the O'odham worked on Spanish or Pima farms, they were paid with flour, seeds, or vegetables. Eventually, ranchers paid them in cash, and the O'odham traveled to trading posts to buy supplies. It became more difficult to share with the entire village. Instead, a man's earnings became his personal savings.

THE SAN XAVIER MISSION WAS BUILT ON TOHONO O'ODHAM LAND IN 1783

The Apache were also changing. Weary of years of battling, they abandoned their raiding, and by 1795 they had moved closer to Spanish forts, where they were given food rations. For a few years, the O'odham and the Apache lived peacefully alongside each other.

In 1821, Mexico declared its independence from Spain. But the new Mexican government was not wealthy enough to supply the Apache. Raiders again attacked O'odham villages, and the Desert People moved farther south to safety near Mexican military posts.

Gadsden Purchase ➤ Antonio Lopez de Santa Anna, the president of Mexico, needed to raise money to run his new country. After long discussions with American General James Gadsden, Santa Anna agreed to sell 29,640 square miles (76,800 sq km) of land for $10 million. The area, which contained nearly all the tribal lands of the Tohono O'odham, passed to the United States.

When the treaty was signed, on June 29, 1854, one-third of the Papaguería became part of Mexico. The rest became American territory. No one discussed the purchase with the Tohono O'odham. Neither the Americans nor the Mexicans ever considered that the land they were bartering had been inhabited by the tribe for centuries.

While the Pima and O'odham remained peaceful, the Apache did not. With help from friendly tribes, the U.S. government confined the Apache to a reservation to encourage white settlements. By 1872, the Apache agreed to a lasting peace.

The O'odham returned to their scattered villages, desert crops, and trade routes. But they wanted

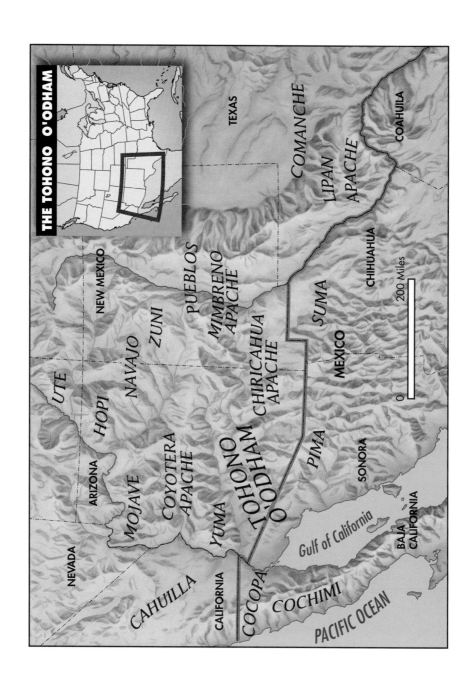

THE TOHONO O'ODHAM

TEXAS

COMANCHE

LIPAN APACHE

COAHUILA

CHIHUAHUA

200 Miles

0

NEW MEXICO

PUEBLOS

MIMBRENO APACHE

SUMA

MEXICO

ZUNI

NAVAJO

UTE

HOPI

CHIRICAHUA APACHE

COYOTERA APACHE

TOHONO O'ODHAM

PIMA

SONORA

ARIZONA

MOJAVE

YUMA

Gulf of California

BAJA CALIFORNIA

NEVADA

CAHUILLA

CALIFORNIA

COCOPA

COCHIMI

PACIFIC OCEAN

protected rights to their land. By 1897, the United States granted them a reservation of slightly more than 111 square miles (290 sq km) around San Xavier del Bac, the site of the first Spanish mission. Shortly thereafter, they were granted an additional area of 35 square miles (90 sq km) at Gila Bend.

Prospectors roaming the desert discovered rich copper, silver, and gold deposits. Others found that the desert offered good grazing land. American mining companies and cattle ranchers established towns, post offices, stagecoach and rail lines, stores, and schools. Some of the Desert People took jobs with the new companies. They built homes with glass windows, woodstoves, dishes, and furniture. But many others moved farther into the desert to preserve their traditional way of life.

The O'odham resented losing their land to growing white settlements. By 1916, they secured more land, raising their total area significantly. Today's combined reservations include some 4,500 square miles (11,600 sq km), about the size of the state of Connecticut. Still, reservation lands are much smaller than the original Papaguería. In 1955, the O'odham secured full mineral rights, allowing them to rent mines to non-native companies. Their reservation is the second largest in the United States. Only the Navajo Nation is larger.

TOHONO O'ODHAM TODAY

Schools ➤ Beginning in the 1890s, many Tohono O'odham children were sent to mission boarding schools, where they learned English and were exposed to non-native ways. When they graduated, nearly everyone "returned to the blanket," meaning they came back to their villages. Many became village leaders. The tribe began to establish its own schools so that children could remain at home.

The first reservation school was established in 1917. Today, the reservations run seven preschools, seven elementary schools, four junior high schools, and three senior high schools. Children study both the Tohono O'odham language and English. They also learn traditional dances. Students from three tribal schools are members of the Indian Oasis Intertribal Dancers, a group that performs at events in many states.

The San Xavier Mission School is a typical reservation elementary school. In addition to regular subjects, it publishes books in the Tohono O'odham language

A FESTIVE PROCESSION IN HONOR OF SAINT FRANCIS
LEAVES THE CHURCH IN TOPAWA, ARIZONA.

and teaches traditional crafts. Each year students participate in an Indian Day celebration. Recently, a native
weaver taught the children basket making. Girls have a
toka team and travel to other villages for matches.

Christianity ➤ The O'odham were among the first
American Indians introduced to Christianity by Jesuit

missionaries. Today, every village has a church, and the people combine ancient traditions with Catholic or Presbyterian services. Each year on October 4, they celebrate the Festival of Saint Francis. Schools are closed and there are special services, followed by a festive procession, music, and song. A village feast with dancing lasts into the night.

Tribal Government ➤ In 1936, the O'odham divided the reservation into eleven districts, with two elected representatives from each district serving on a Tribal Council. They drew up a constitution that was approved by a popular vote. The Council established headquarters in Sells, Arizona, where a modern building now houses offices for many tribal services.

Mexican O'odham ➤ The southern O'odham lost most of their land to the Mexican government. In 1927, after many legal difficulties, the tribe was granted a small reservation. In 1979, the Tribal Council in Sells petitioned the Mexican government on behalf of their tribal cousins and won two additional village reservations. They also obtained permission for members to travel freely across the border. They are now asking the United States to grant dual citizenship to Mexican O'odham, so that they can obtain needed health care and social services from American government and tribal agencies.

Work ➤ In 1933, President Franklin D. Roosevelt established a national Civilian Conservation Corps (CCC) to provide jobs during the difficult time of the Great Depression. Tribal leaders decided which projects were most needed, and the CCC trained tribe members to do these tasks. O'odham teams built wells for drinking water, excavated charcos with power machinery, and brought in electrical and tele-

THE TOHONO O'ODHAM LEARNED MANY SKILLED JOBS IN THE 1930S AND 1940S THAT THEY CONTINUE TODAY, SUCH AS MINING.

phone lines. They also built roads, and soon cars and trucks brought villages closer together.

During World War II, many Tohono O'odham entered military service. Military duty brought them to parts of the world they had never seen. Their experiences and job training took them far from their villages. Many men who did not enter the military worked in factories and mines to produce materials needed for the war, and some did not return to family ranches.

Today, O'odham men and women work at jobs both on and off the reservation. Many go to college and have careers in teaching, nursing, medicine, and law. Others work in skilled jobs for mining companies, government agencies, factories, and ranches. Kitts Peak Observatory uses reservation land for astronomy research and employs many tribe members. Also, O'odham work for themselves as farmers, cattle ranchers, artists, basket weavers, and business owners.

The tribe runs several enterprises that provide jobs and income, including mines and a casino. Profits from the casino fund a college scholarship for O'odham students. In return for assistance, each student agrees to work on a reservation for about two years after graduation, giving back to the tribe the skills and expertise they gain.

Tourism also gives members of the tribe a chance to work and introduce their culture to others. Travelers visit the San Xavier del Bac Mission, the historic church

THE TOHONO O'ODHAM CONTINUE TO MAKE
BEAUTIFUL CRAFTS IN THE TRADITIONAL MANNER,
SUCH AS THIS GLAZED POT.

that has been used by the O'odham for more than two
hundred years. The annual Tohono O'odham All-Indian
Rodeo brings visitors who watch skilled riders in com-
petitive events and browse in stalls along the fairgrounds
that offer native baskets, pottery, and food. Above all,
the Desert People continue to preserve their traditions
and pass them on. There are now about 15,000 members of the tribe, and the Tohono O'odham continue to
live in harmony with their desert lands.

GLOSSARY

Adobe A brick made of clay and straw, used to build some desert houses.

Agave A low desert plant with sharp, pointed leaves. The leaves could be stripped for their strong fibers, which were used to make rope.

Arroyo A sandy stream bed that is dry during times of drought and filled with flowing water after heavy rain.

Beargrass A wild herb used for food and also dried for use in weaving baskets.

Cactus A desert plant with shallow roots, sharp spines, and the ability to store water.

Cactus camp Temporary camp sites built among the saguaro cactus when it was time to harvest the cactus fruit.

Charco A low area in the desert that holds rainwater.

Cholla A low, spiny cactus that produces red fruit each autumn.

Creosote bush A desert bush that blooms with yellow flowers each spring.

Devil's claw A black claw-shaped shrub often dried and woven into baskets.

Head-bearers Men who wore deer headdresses as a disguise when they hunted deer.

Mesquite tree A low-growing desert tree that produces pods containing small black beans.

Metate A stone used for grinding corn, wheat, or dried beans into flour.

Ocotillo A tall, thin cactus often used for building fences and houses.

Olla A clay jug made in various sizes and mostly used to store water and keep it cool.

Pavi O'odham Pima name referring to the Tohono O'odham tribe, meaning "the Bean People."

Pinole A food made of ground corn or mesquite beans mixed with water.

Ramada An open area with a thatched roof attached to desert houses. The Desert People worked and ate under its shade and often slept under it on warm nights.

Saguaro Name of a cactus that grows as tall as 50 feet (15 m) and produces a sweet red fruit.

Tohono O'odham Official name of the tribe, meaning "The Desert People."

Toka A game similar to modern field hockey, played by girls and women.

Viikita A harvest celebration held once every four years by Pima and Tohono O'odham tribes.

Yucca A plant with long, sharp leaves that can be dried and woven into baskets.

FOR MORE INFORMATION

Baylor, Boyd. *The Desert Is Theirs*. New York: Aladdin Books, 1987.

Erickson, Winston P. *Sharing the Desert: The Tohono O'odham in History*. Tucson: University of Arizona Press, 1994.

Landau, Elaine. *The Hopi*. New York: Franklin Watts, 1994.

Nabhan, Gary Paul. *The Desert Smells Like Rain*. San Francisco: North Point Press, 1982.

Powell, Suzanne. *The Pueblos*. New York: Franklin Watts. 1993.

Tohono O'odham: Lives of the Desert People. Sells, Ariz.: Tohono O'odham Education Department, 1984.

Underhill, Ruth. *Papago Woman*. Prospect Heights, Ill.: Waveland Press, 1985.

Waldman, Carl. *Word Dance*. New York: Facts on File, 1994.

Internet Sites

Due to the changeable nature of the Internet, sites appear and disappear very quickly. Internet addresses must be entered exactly as they appear.

The **Yahoo** directory of the World Wide Web is an excellent place to find Internet sites on any topic. The directory is located at:

http://www.yahoo.com

The Heard Museum of Native Cultures and Art in Phoenix, Arizona, contains descriptions of and links to many educational resources on the Indians of the Southwest United States:

http://www.heard.org/index.htm

The Arizona ThemeMall contains a guide to the tribes and reservations of the Southwest United States and promotes the American Indian perspective on their own history:

http://thememall.com/tribes/indians.html-ssi#list

INDEX

Italicized page numbers indicate illustrations.

ABOUT THE AUTHOR

Jacqueline Dembar Greene worked as a reporter and feature writer for several years before she turned to writing for young people full time. Her picture book, *Butchers and Bakers, Rabbis and Kings,* was a finalist for the National Jewish Book Award. Her historical novel, *Out of Many Waters,* and its companion, *One Foot Ashore,* were both named Sydney Taylor Honor Books. She has just completed her newest historical novel, *Miguel, Son of Abraham,* which tells the story of a young Mexican-American boy and a Tohono O'odham youth who share their lives as they try to survive in the Arizona desert.

Mrs. Greene has a B.A. in French Literature from the University of Connecticut and an M.A. in English Literature from Central Missouri University. She enjoys hiking, traveling, and photography, and some of her photos appear in this book. She has traveled extensively in the American Southwest and the Yucatan Peninsula of Mexico, and she has visited numerous Native American sites.